exits / origins

by

NIKKI DUDLEY

THE KNIVES FORKS AND SPOONS PRESS
NEWTON-LE-WILLOWS

Published in the United Kingdom in 2010
by The Knives Forks And Spoons Press,
10 Avocet Close,
Newton-le-Willows,
Merseyside,
WA12 9RE.

ISBN 978-1-907812-09-5

Thanks to Joe, Trini, Jeff Hilson, and Peter Jaeger.

Thanks to these publications for publishing single poems from this collection: *Streetcake*, *The Delinquent*, *etcetera art blogspot*.

When writing exits/origins, I followed two rules:

1. Don't close the poems

2. Start with something overheard, seen out and about, repetitive phrases or something I stumbled across by chance.

CONTENTS

Northbound

you?   The book told
lies when I picked it up, when
the bed   carried me away that

night, you disappeared
and I dreamt lost
the eyes, the mouth. Keep

thinking of him, you,
tired journeys, restless lines
of colour
          taking back

to nothing.
              Writing on trains where ink
              is smudged and spied,
              secrets spilt like vomit,

people are crowded
and intrigued.

He said, 'stop stressing about
everything', saw lies telling
lives

when I woke. I knew he must have

looked down, said hello

ASKING THEM TO GUESS.

The last page
                              is written. I saw the covers and ducked, expecting
bombs. The character was stained
from birth, it slithered between words / and /paragraphs without
anyone tracking its foul smell. It was a smudge on
a window, blurring / the details

            inthetrees, the/buildings, andespec/iallythelights.

            The glass exploded when
the sounds rumbled together to make tru/th. It threw me out

of dreams and left me

staring at the r/ed numbers, afraid to turn on
the lights and see

            the room   turning / back.

Keep rereading the beginning= keep the
eyes from rolling. Saw our future and
                  pressed   *PAUSE.*

I gave things labels to excuse
their ugliness. The labels were spilt wro/nge and they peeled off in old age and eventu/ally were

discharged to duty *a pole it/ truths*
that are easy to bury but you can't
bury me, or the print, ed. pages

you can't buried me shaking in the morning shaping up the month with a pen and a number/ squashed
with the wait for escarpment:

working on this age.

Fuck so satisfying when writhing in words/dialogue that scars underneath
the sound of ringing, I think about what they dreamt about and the empty notebook,

aside: secret verses
about love?

The hedge shook in sympathy when the balloon hit the twigs, and we all fall down, we all feel drowned,
ringing words in my ears to say hello

-Is that all you want? Is that the means to errand?

The ghostly vision haunts him like the blank pages, a yawn that stretches for 49 sheets until he
scratches the words 'these blank pages represent

the rest of my life'

and I'm sore, no *sure*, the pole it never dries/ ink drips from the fingertips
when curtains gather, my love. Imagine the blessed balloon is fit to burp, a stammer into your
consciousness, that falling
                    man.

A name represents a fate? Don't take it literary or fate becomes your 'name' / lean back / hold your
nose / submerge memory in the blush of the names on the arches – scratch my own I'll scratch my own
in the notebook where

sigh lent louder than protest = HE UNFURNISHED

Ich bin frei oh lie down next to my

words and scream

streams of emotions wrap around my legs you around my legs

-the wiry eyesight of boredom / flashing /

Four Moments.

In the lamplight of starlight, star, star, stare at stars but

it felt infinite

once, 'freedom's a joke' bitter eyes, mine is a strong

once, and I hope death

isn't closer now

Pull the covers over, pull the covert over!

The sweat of sex is like tears of the bodies, twisting and tearing and teeth chewing

on the edges of queue, wait the line, weight lines in tens experiences

leave a message, wear

TWO MINUTES ...

Took the veins-tied
a r i b b o n a r o u n d m y n e c k
alveoli jerked whaled a sudden car crash bent
beached wreckage corks swelled filled the hole where
my throat tongue lungs wrapping rubbing hair between your

f i n g e r s g a u z y   tapestry preserve you in a

                                        tomb smother oxygen tree

                                        snapped in the garden hands had

                                        a scent of softness as you tighten grip

                                        trying to eat the world can't swallow

                                        emptiness ribbon is a scar that can hardly

                              be seen umbilical cord now cut

                    from the source can kill when

            the car was spinning I believed

    y o u   w o u l d   t h a w

        the ice but the pores in my lungs are

    frozen can the wheels stop spinning

  release from inevitable turn in churn blue blood that blossoms behind your skin

  with time colder then ice colder than asphyxiation applied finger by finger bye

* 09 *

**"The sky is turning itself
in side, out,"** you said

and the cars were barriers to our escape.

The sky flapped like a (bird) caught in
                                    my mouth tasted like blood

as I looked up to check: turning/ plastic bodies rolling over.

EYE IMAGINE the what are, what are you looking
at stranglers? Please hold my hand.

"It scares me," you said, flipping an eye shut/ drive towards
Ex- but don't, please don't, let the tyres scream

Won't jump out/hold on
Won't jump on/hold out

Want to wake up in the darkness and know you're a life, or is it beating, beating
fortune?

Call

Fuck I won'ted to fuck you

up? Or some other way, maybe mint

something else but can't change how they

reeds this. It's words that I love and worse
that I hat – don't finish that –

put it on, girl...

This city, swirling with ashen faces, think off
something, something thinks of you, wanna

be sum one's someone.   (You still in?

Take the river awry and we swim in cement, and that hurts
the arms and hurts my legs. There's met hood to this
mad hearse...

Method and we kissed, among the mirage that was
rubble, but who stares/ when   you are
                                    standing
                                              right

Control Alt Delete I'm starting
over I'm starting

over there, a sheep spray painted red is my imagination
playing ticks or am I

starting over, the words are fucking at the back
wards of lonely people waiting for visiting hours

to end, am I starting

Control deleted by a finger / I'm over
in a hurdle, comma hurdle, trapping me

-Words worse for where, my favourite town?

You are a beacon, and let's start at
seven, sever the ties of 9-6 and wear bin bags instead and if I Alternate
between yes and maybe, can we dance over

hot colds to Delete 'I'm' and leave we
to star to veer because it's not the sentence I wanted to be, it's not
the page that I saw written in my head, but if I roll over will I

be a journalist instead, will I forget your love and feel alone, will I put com,mas in the
wrong places, will I backwards walk and wear tracksuits, will I peel labels off bottles,
will eye press Control, Alt and forget Delete, willow

drown me by a river without

"LET'S HAVE SEX LIKE BANANAS"

A voice drifted across the smell of cunning trees,

and the river flickered like a blaze trying to disguise them.

> You looked me in the eye and I understood your pupils were full/ stopped and
> remembered how lost we could have been without these fences.

The letters were always friends and constantly networked at social occasions,
interchanging, swapping/ the edge of

                                        colours that makers shake an eye

I don't know quite why, finger squeezing my heart the universe tripped its mouth

over for you... When standing on the receding

glacier, my eyes were scarred invisibly and I say   'I'd keep them'

to stop wandering eyes, when words and cheeks are only
brimming with colours.

Will you ever, sea of tears? Overthrowing the bridge the others stood

on for safety, looking across at the sunset, the hiccupping

stars but, all you feel is the warmth

gradually diminishing.

Yet, no light, no

lights?

Finger squeezing my heart- I'd die

if you

let

EVERY PIECE OF FURNITURE TELLS A

Life, sitting in this chair, turning red.

Squares of dark nest grow like an extended tear

Please, ask

When we young, the future bright...

Now the dimmer switches are turning down

the sunshine, the earth is rolling into a cavern and

the light spreads like a hand stretching

towards the non-planet that they have

taken from our rhymes. I know you are   there between

the slats, trying to reach me when I'm dreaming of explosions

and routine, when the streetlights are humming alone in the half-light,

the cold congregating LIKE TEARS on my eye/ lift crayon drawings

from the pavement that is staring at the *sky*>>>>>>>>>>>>>

lies to the futile FOLDS the stomach, eating straw and gold, will

we sink in the monsoon? Can't remember the last scorch...

as strong as alcohol on a bleeding **Wound Abyss** Reminds

me of the dreams- 1.falling 2.fall in 3.fool him 4.find sin full

words and scratch them on the windows, the walls,

wind them around your feet until you can't walk

left or correct. Why the sky? Why not the floor

that leads us to voices who are speaking

in "languages" and codes? The mark

sto

ryin

and

thes

storm in a sea

makes me **uncertain** but I

told him twist dial to the

right twice, then left

until it clicks, then

ust **enter**

t he numb-

Hi all!

As if you taught me how to hop again in the middle

of hurricanes and punch tuition, I lost the

stop.

That cancer beating your chest like a second

heart like nothing ever lived when people lined

upwards to see/speak/scratch and no one

        heard in the dark the soul in tune /

        the light of death.

Across London, scanning words to find the tears in the day
for love, you emailed me between the madness and monotony and mould >

right soon,

we'll write this soon but weight in your cheeks
much rosier now

I can't turn you white again, with the powder of pounds ground
our hearts, hold on, put them in a pile and we'll start

a gain feels like something and nothing

when I think about white spaces, white spaces and   right foolishness
I never seen you

Blood in my
ear can you heave me gorgeous? What you say about me huh?
When you said I'm a chore, only soft rumbles, blood dried
and tested tissue paper wrestling did you
here and now?

It's all solid   a promise?

Didn't hiss a word you said, I saw your lips
I saw blood on my nail like copper plating and these ears

drowning.

Call me later when the night has vomited on light. Close my eyes and you
lit up my brain

blood melted, every day, blues melted

and no fucking stars

**id I buy this small
otepad because my thoughts are now
mall?**

he space made my mind seem like
 stream winding
etween
ountains. Hot pools

oil my thoughts whilst I sit in air-
onditioned

 boxes.

                                                offices, surrounded by pens

nused pens are prison bars, only hinting
 freedom when I let
e ink cascade onto paper/ snarling
 the blurry screen until the words revolt/
ssolve.

riting is graffiti between 9am-6pm.
                                           I could be
                                        detained for
                                   vandalism/time
                                 wasting/causing
                                      a public
                                 disturbance/
                                     slander...

et the words scramble
n the page to burst the lines
oon lines of justified
pe written
                   blocks

A DIFF
E RENT
PROB
LEM

a pre
sent to
myself.

street-woke
to sound of
trees, whining

rain twining
around the tacky
film of skin

numbers keep
building like
harvested snow
that never melts.

the gadgets tried
to dig us from the
formality of
existence but letter
heads weighed on
the snow, con

my feet, and sigh
couldn't

a different
problem and
yet another,
and the colour
of the sky
a bruised banana,

forced into
candle light,
hum onwards
one wards full
like gutters

prescribed words should
fucking burn

have to keep
typing rapidly
or the glue will
dry, my fingerprints
will merge with the
letters, no real lease

buildings join
hands and cry
glass into the
drink moving towards

lisp. this is
the last sing I
expected as light
closed its eyes is
it clearer
now? or now?
a few seconds
have passed, and
now

precision is a
compass carving into
my mind details
like grain on
a tree trunk, precision
has a history, a number
of complex
and interweaving
relationships, who am I

two snap the skip
in rope who ham eye

MY VERY LIFE

LIVED my igloo breath built

WALLS from the strangers- drunk/
shivering by the signs, pointing both

ways. My arch enemy in ink. Ink the darkness

of the month, the light a quiet note separated
from the voice of springs. Too

nostalgic, but humans awwwww, hum ands
are creating creations.

The misty spaghetti cereal in unknown
streets, I asked him

where yell oh, wear home

IS THE TREASON FOR METAPHOR.

    a) Put you in a cell to stop the genocide.
    b) Change your hair colour
    c) Switch those recognisable clothes.
    d) Alter that wonky smile
    e) Wear some coloured contacts oar

runs… Lips are putty too

words entering/exiting/escaping. Can't hide you in
the search engine where
they will skin you to the frame.

Enter the witness protection program;

      we can make you appear as a simile, an adjective, a compound-verb even and
we can use you still in private meetings in basements, in notes passed on the train in
    rush hour, whilst we dream in our beds, mouthing you as we walk to the beat.

This is language
lobotomy, this is elimination
of the 'better' opponent. Come with
me to my secret annex and we won't flush, we'll use
the books to veil us, we'll whisper in the
torch light, we'll instead use clichés like

walking on egg

HOW IT WORKS:

two hundred leaves could burrow

the things i meant to say but squashed under my tee-

th the past has forgotten how the gravel was marked with the tiring tracks

(did the flowers start to grow when we heard about you?

is it all
connected
like the blood
circulation
system

the mountain is smaller in my mind but
bigger in the dreams

i am sliding into
the envelope

see all outside darkness did I
sleep did I call you or was the night

out. Reel me inside before the rain solidifies
hard like marbles
pulping me like eyes
squashed   against   bricks.

Explosions
look like umbrellas?   They led us with the lights

of their mobile phones, modern mime

out an exit wound out of site out of mine
the drone will   continue to burn
why did we stop evolving?

        Umbrella explosions?
Marbles as white as cowardice/ Led. Lured.

A wire clamping the neck, they led us,

pulping bricks into granules 'Woah, I almost forgot
this was on your...' cheese crammed
into the cracks

                                                                    fool

SO I'M NOT SPEAKING ENGLISH NOW

the bricks are full of air and the cracks erupt a tear in
the skin, the organs swelling and pushing up the cells like bubbles,
transparent speech marks rising in the air, transporting whispers
of what you said to push me down like cigarette ends a life, alphabet suits, jumble of
accusations and silence steaming like vegetables, all goods evaporated. Knees burning
from the dynamite I spread on the floor, hoping the heel would spark as it swung
towards my head, an axe that avoids the clean cut snip of poison congregating in
vessels, snaking towards the left-brain, discolouring thoughts like bleach. Everything
is brown. The smell of the clean bed sheets, the night air from the window, the
clucking of the key, bored. The lock groans when I arrive and shouts-
when all leave I ate the papers that build a vessel
to trap me, to drag me from your outstretched hand,
s o m e w h e r e   o v e r
L o n d o n ,   r a p e
me of the papers

that flow together

like chains

CAKE. My niece would eat it all.

A beginning

four words? The mountains grave only

                 fragments

                 and dust.

The ice streams of pressure

           filtering away

                                    from the holes.

                           The tongue transforms twists
                           and says nothing.

Cutting out   heart   is a surgical procedure, there are no hostages

in the tissue. This is
        peace of
        line wrap
           ping

BATHING CELLS: sickness leading
             too depression leading too

                              lyricist throw a life ring

in middle of silence, run down
in a country road- solitude at it's
loneliest singing merrily about failing flowers, the rain

                              weighing
                              my coat
                              bathing cells underneath.

             Woken by intravenous needle, catching
             like a hook. My lip
             is curled upwards in a sneer but
             I mean to smile. What did? An intravenous

                                                  route to the city,

way back delayed, being engineered for future use,
dark the twang of his voice, sickly fruit
that stings and rejuvenates. Is this

good for the good fore bode in shells for God miss this

"I'm going to fuck your brother!"

On the application, hand
written is a convict *shaky*
shadowy cons ripped off that
elderly woman. Cowards are the loudest animals
and muscle their parts into

                                 spaces   holes

I can't think on applications / the quest tonnes
get shaving- will they come
back?

I'm going to tell you about *hippopotamuses* and spell innit enough.
The font is **shouting** but the people
can't see, the people are untroubled
by the paper it is written on write on whilst
the city giggles over the buildings your
hair groans wetter.

I'm going to fuck luck, or yuck
fuck, or muck truckers who
aren't your brother.

Colder hands massage heart: are you dyed? Are
you in deed? Spaces filled
with black thoughts that in a different light
look red. Will their clothes
be crawling with

PURPOSE BEYOND PROFITS. Prose fits a

round the winding cluck did you hear the

new news? I refreshed your head with

my brrrringing don't leave me hanging

on the tell a foam in my ears – your lips

moving but I am not.

Yellow is the most beautiful ream

minds are darker when I saws you running but then

nowhere asked my name/ my name?

Ask the bright faced one, he nude, he nude so much

that I had to kill him. Yes, it hurts in the morphing at

7:22 I dreamt of shots, but was it you was it me was it them was it worse hit was the

sky drip

ping onto my eyes with lead.

Wake up before   wake up

BLINK/plan

A novel when the world is yellow, fuck- I'm yellow like a rain

bowing at twenty-four. Booing 747 times whilst queuing for a job-

lest we forget, less we forfeit when we grow

in bedrooms thinking of growing, turning into orgasms

when leaving, split sextion

love, I'm sorry I forgot to get the meat out, I was running

The darkness of childhood is a scar on my pupil/ people peer

insignia on the life of my line, I rotate a line, a circle?

The boxes are triangles incognito, you are a box incognito with

i's and knows is, yeah, you is boat I full gouge us-

I plan, you blink and it's en –

DRINKERS FOR.

Paper fainting, a yawn with due care, a piss
in the snow. The decision you made about your
name will snag on my mind forever.

The head, liars, that take us to the clocks. Watching the space shrink
with monstrous shadows, boats, rocks until we are sunk.

If we needed proofs, I would chase you past the second paragraph and hop over the
exclamation mark. Push the letters back together and watch them merge into numbers
and equations and answers and formulaic oddities.

The speed bump on your chin that leaves me fined. You flick the
indicators alight and I know which side you're on / distances
that pucker towards us, then horizons spurt and we have to crane the neck.

Long poems, if I had anything particularly long to say.

The smashed mirror I never believed in, plucking each splinter between fat pulsing
fingers and it nicked me, in spite

LIMB   less   luck

Can the kidneys

scope? You could love them like I love   you, could putt the

plug back in, rescue the body before it transforms

in two/ a carcass drowning onboard

a ship, flopping to death

from level ground, (remember: those feet are perfect for

stand ins).   Lust lacquer clocks can

never keep time, did legs go   clockwise or
counter

argue edit is the arched enemy, the shadow that fills the life

boat with **helium**, above you fold as

expected? I say

EACH FULL STOP= shut her.

When we spoke about light, I fell off
ends of sent tenses. Can't read

words with eyes
closed (not because
I can't writ.

The words have foamed on
        both sides,
multiplying in water like
transparency. My eyes are covered
in transparency.

The pen worked until it coughed
            spots, no longer

rested on

        fingers
                    correctly.

                        How could your forgive? How could your
                                forget the turning of the

lever nothing / two is luck.

Broken knows, can't smell

your bullshit

at lease- mine